SIMPLIFIED CLASSICS

FOR PIANO

65 EASY TO PLAY MASTERPIECES

...nged by Marc...

CARL FISCHER®
62 Cooper Square, New York, NY 10003

ATF105

ISBN 0-8258-0347-0

Foreword

Now everyone can play and enjoy the music by the world's greatest composers. The arrangements, although simplified, have a full sound and capture the spirit of the original composition.

These piano solos can be played by musicians of all ages; by musicians who play everyday, once a week, or once a year!
For the MODERNS: Bartók, Kabalevsky, Prokofiev and more!
For the IMPRESSIONISTS: Debussy and Ravel.
For the ROMANTICS: Beethoven, Chopin, Liszt, Tchaikovsky and more!
For the CLASSICAL: Clementi, Haydn, Mozart.
So — pull up that piano bench and play through two centuries of music.

The Publisher

Table of Contents

Sonatina

MUZIO CLEMENTI, Op. 36, No. 1

Quite fast (in two, ♩ = 106)

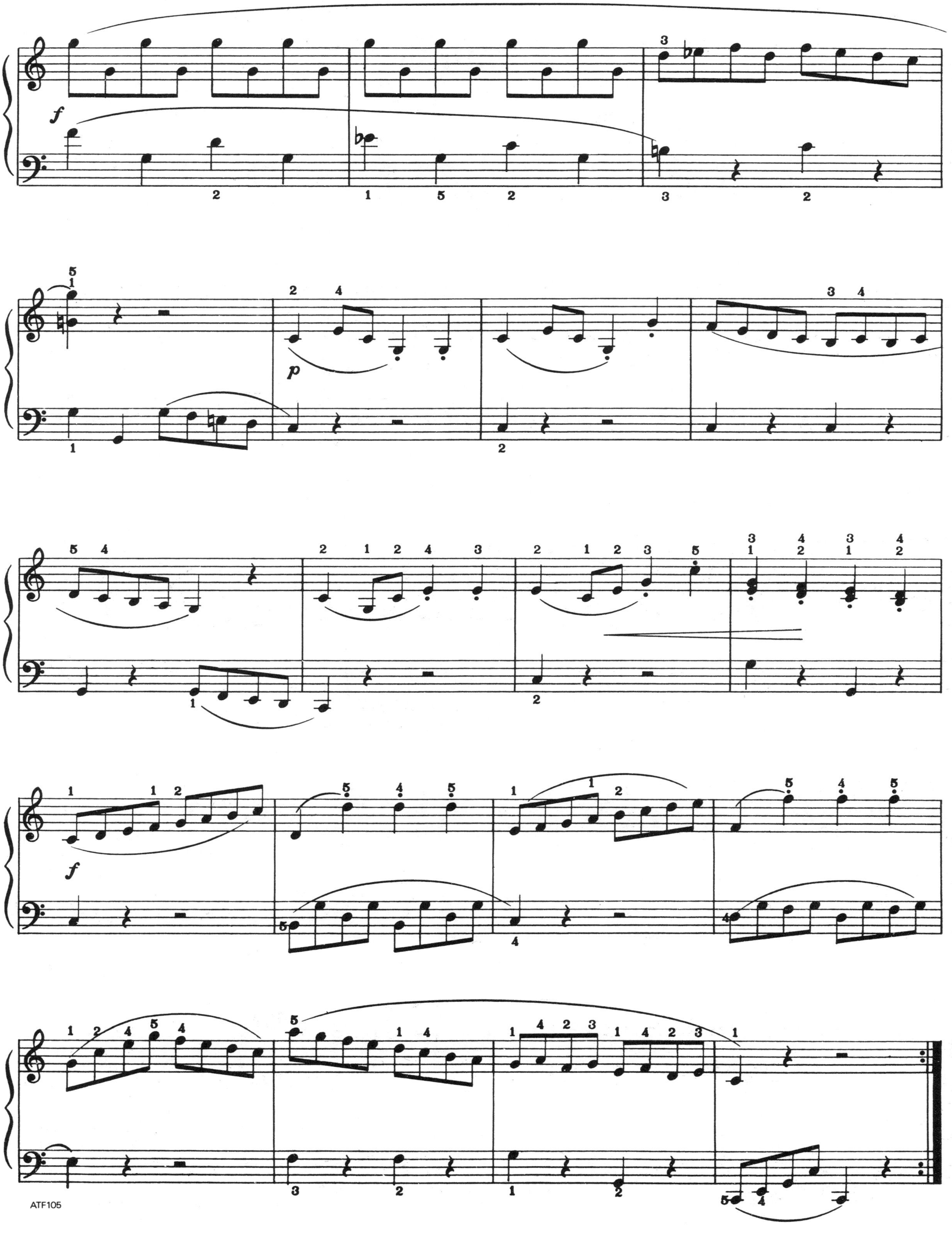
f
p
f

Sonatina

MUZIO CLEMENTI, Op. 36, No. 2

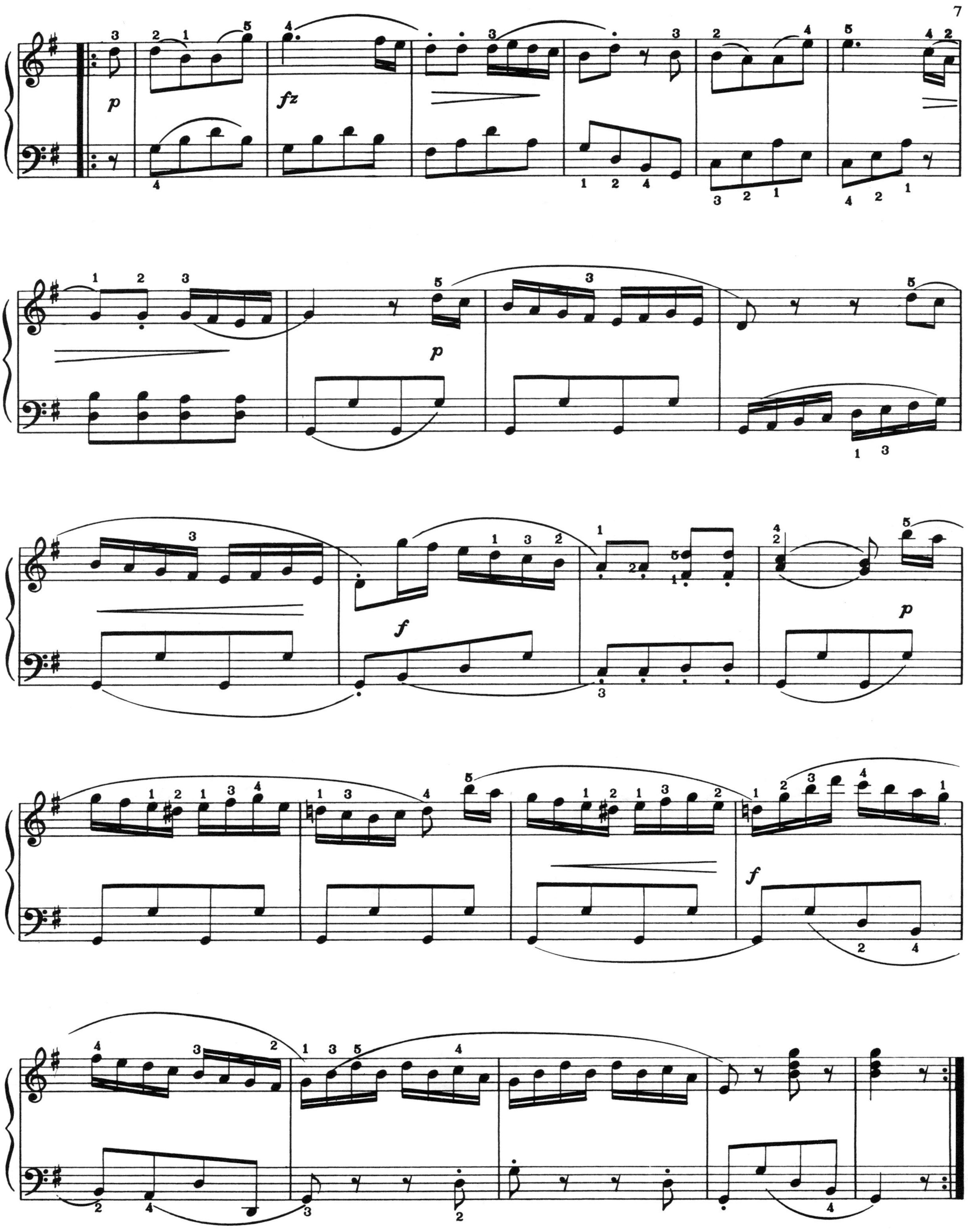

p
fz
f

Sonatina

MUZIO CLEMENTI, Op. 36, No. 3

Moderately fast (♩ = 132)

ATF105

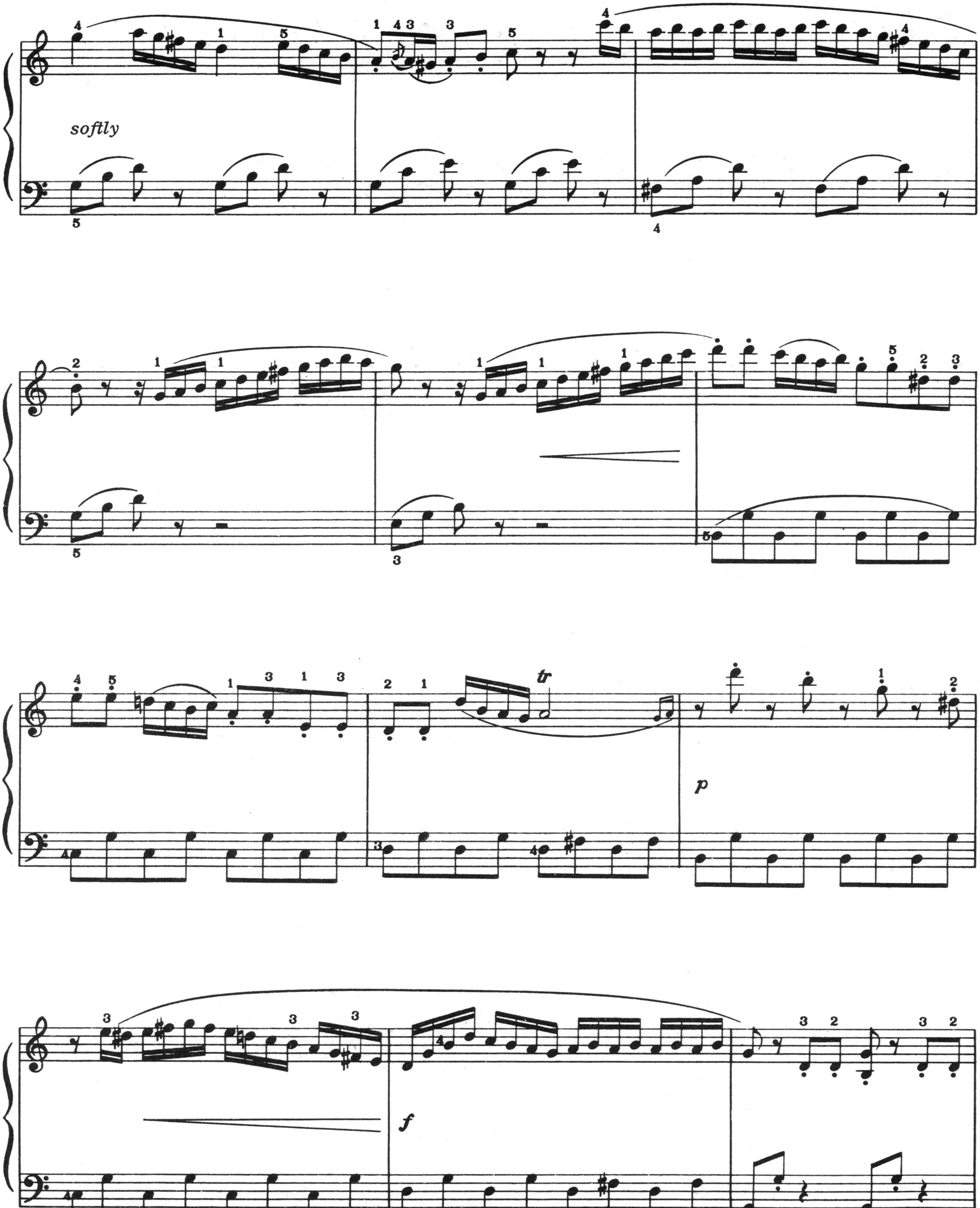
softly
tr
p
f

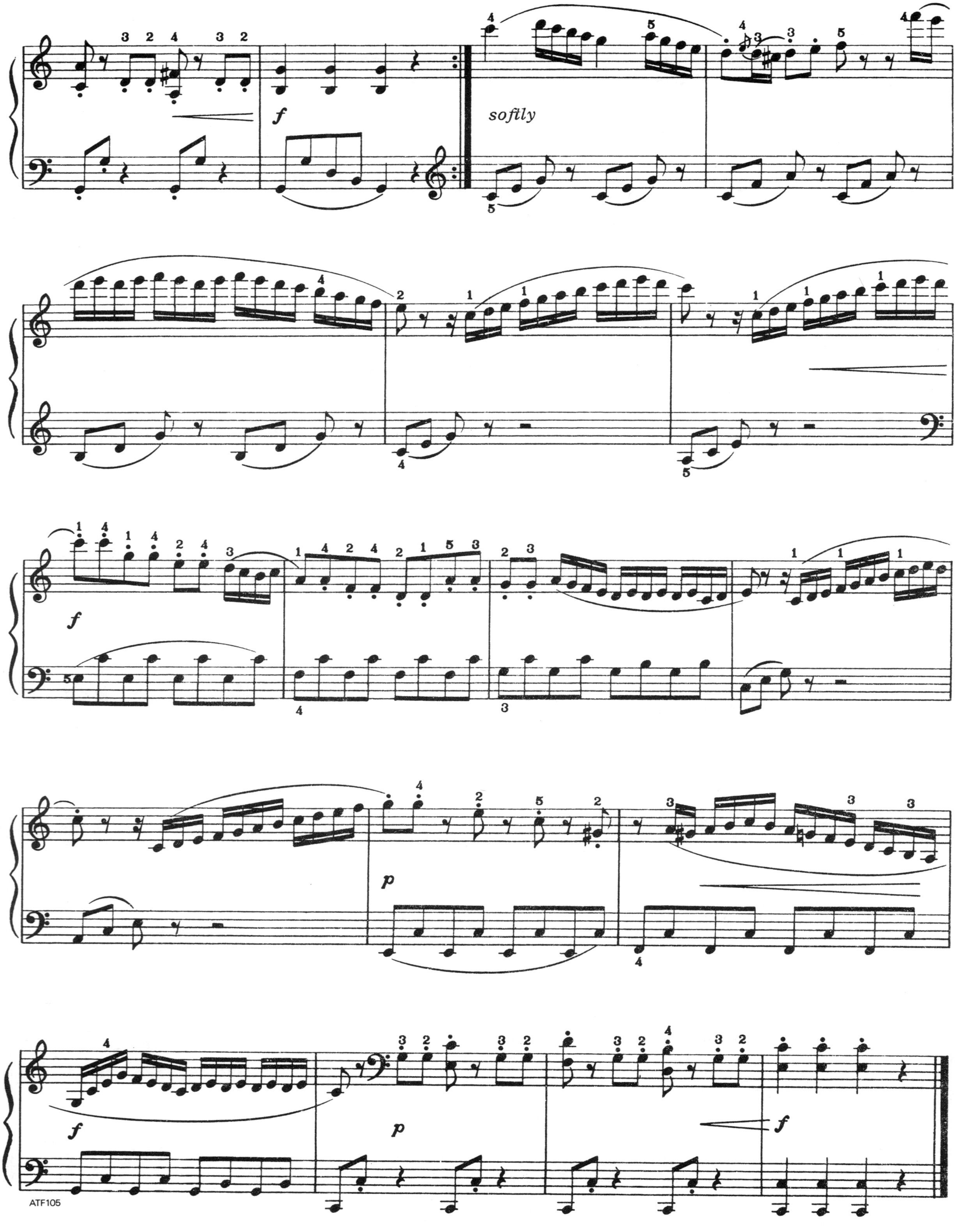
softly
f
p
f
p
f

Sonatina

MUZIO CLEMENTI, Op. 36, No. 4

Moderately fast (♩ = 120)

ATF105

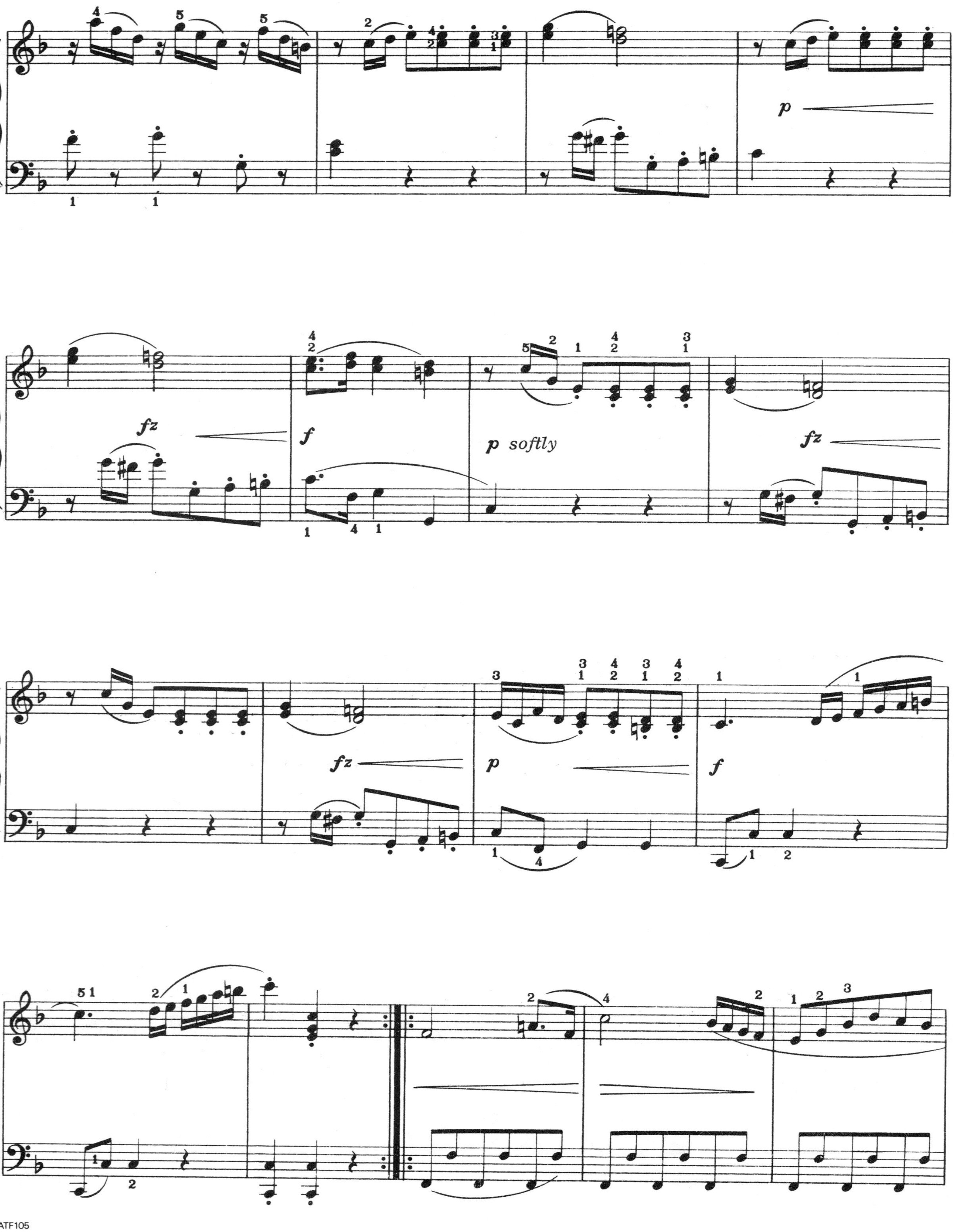
p
fz
f
p softly
fz
fz
p
f

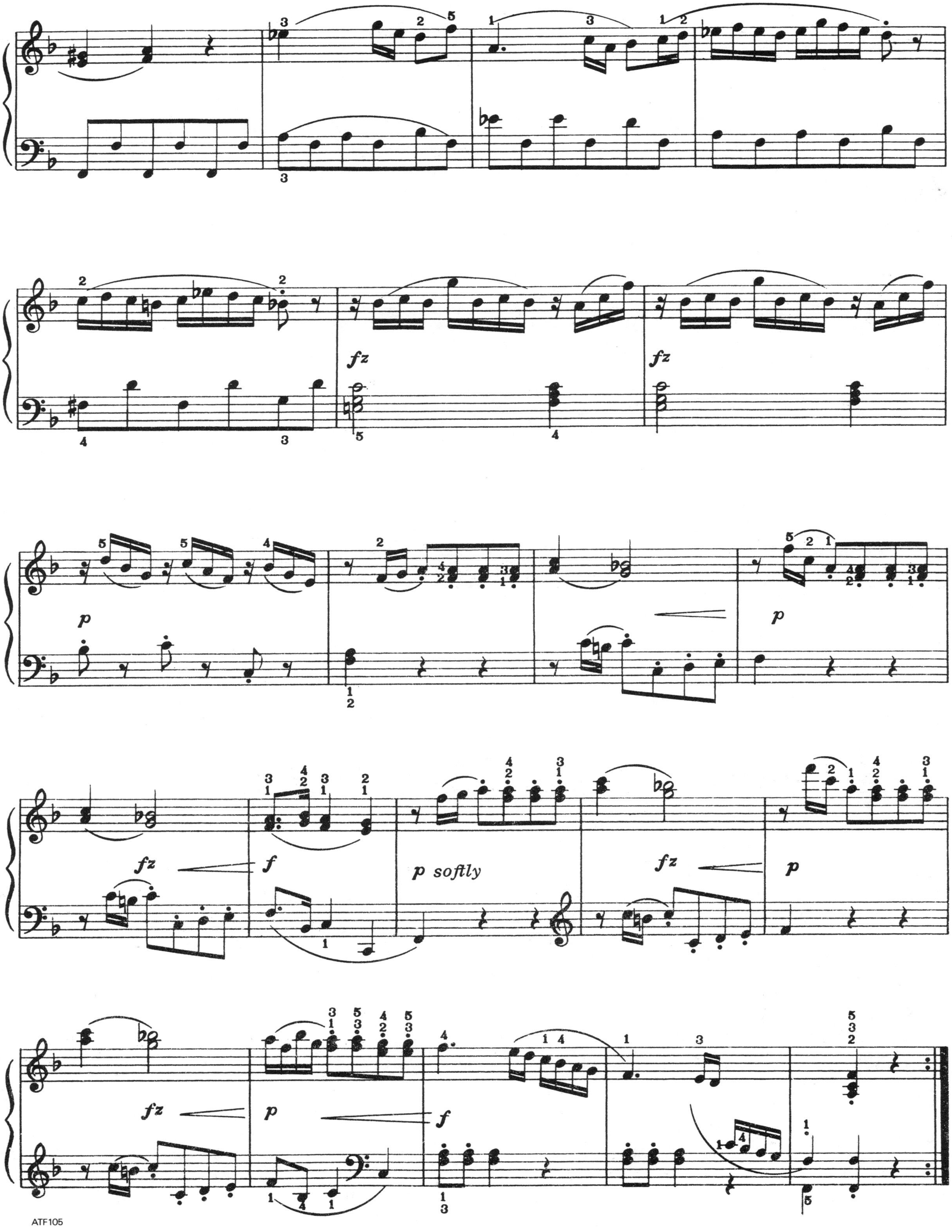
fz
fz
p
p
fz
f
p softly
fz
p
fz
p
f

Sonatina

MUZIO CLEMENTI, Op. 36, No. 5

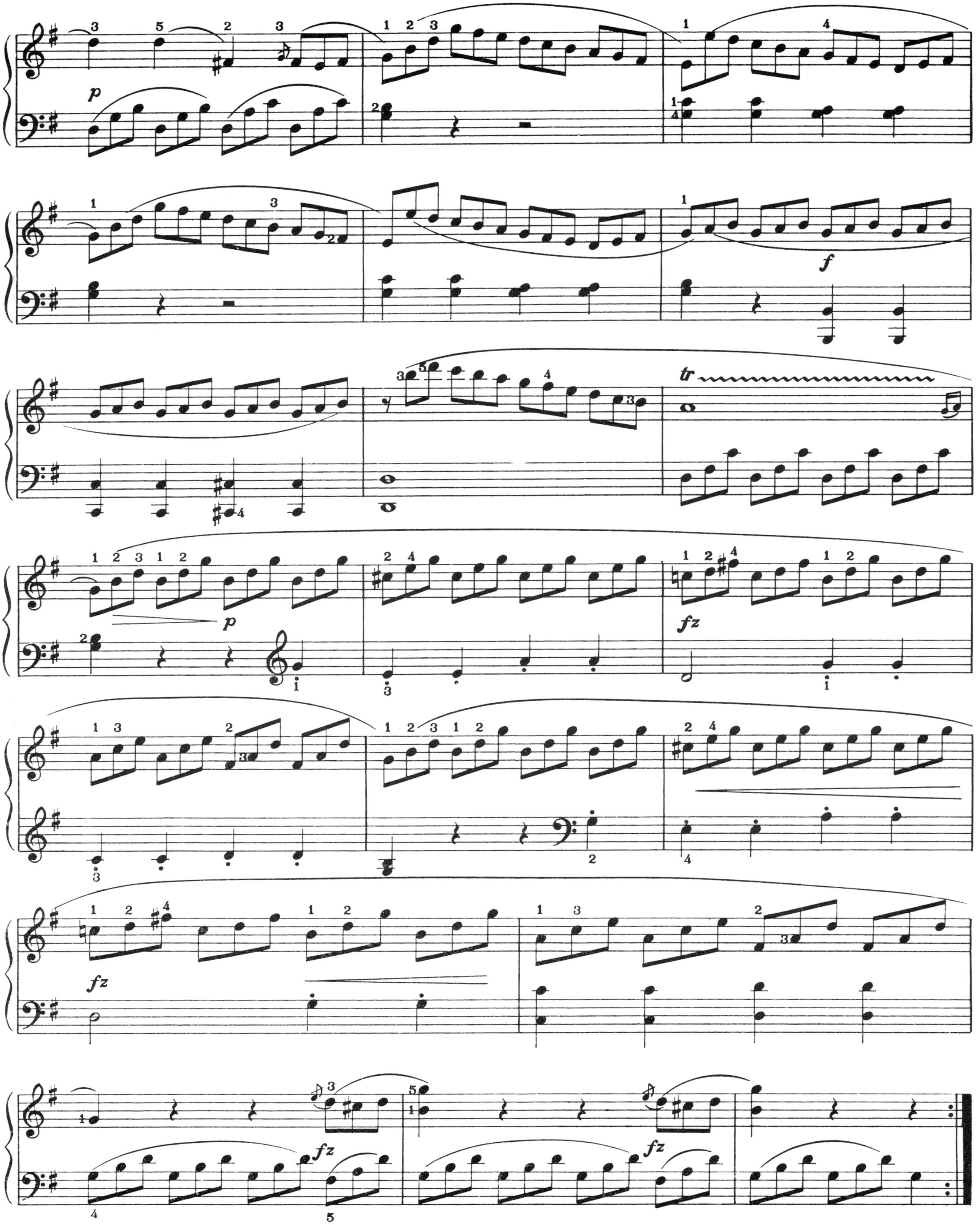
p
f
tr
p
fz
fz
fz
fz

Sonatina

MUZIO CLEMENTI, Op. 36, No. 6

Moderately fast (♩ = 120)

ATF105

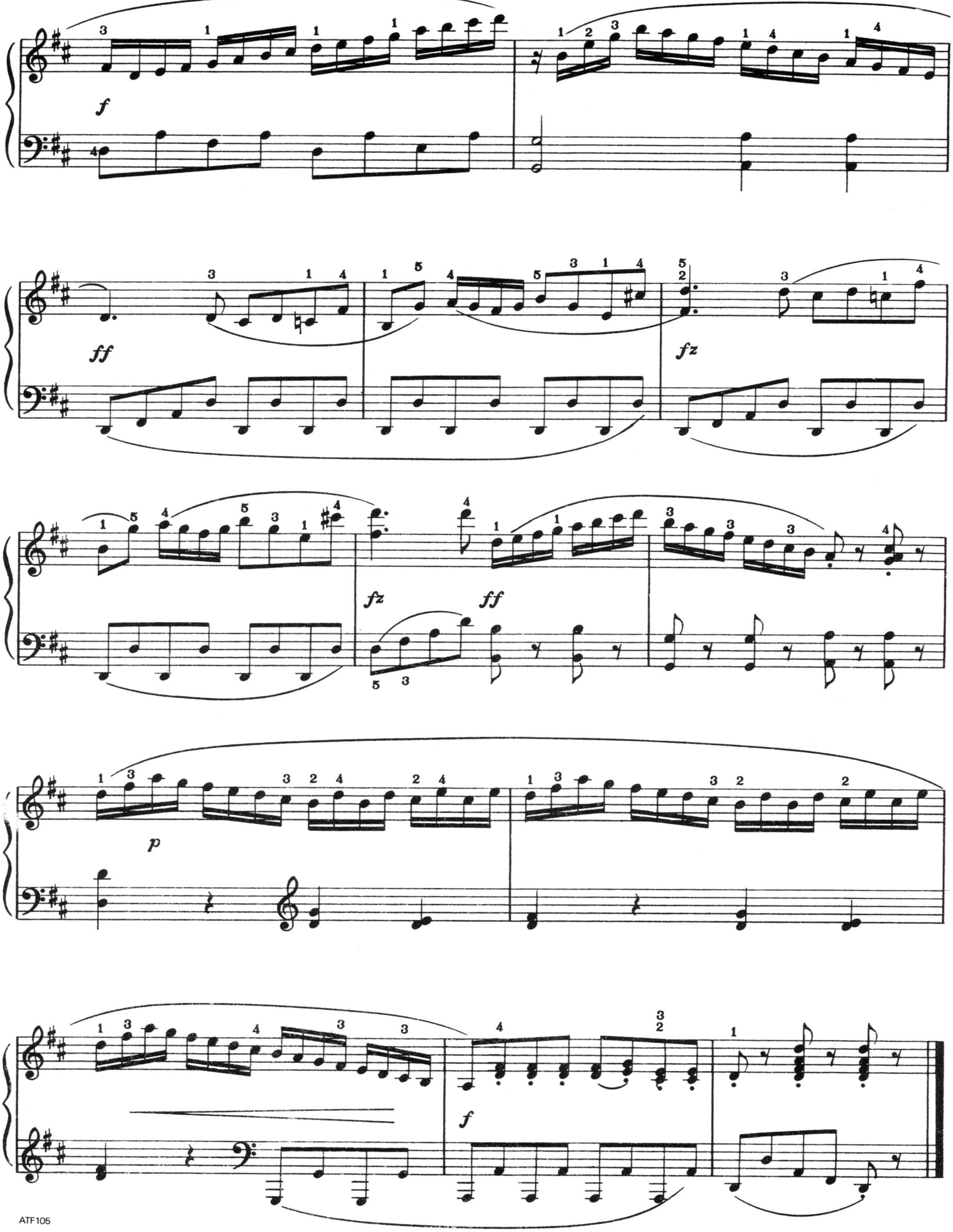
f
ff
fz
fz
ff
p
f

Concerto in D Major

(Theme)

JOSEPH HAYDN

Fast (♩ = 132)

p
p
p
p
f

8va

"Surprise" Symphony

(Theme)

JOSEPH HAYDN

Moderately Slow (♩ = 63)

p
p
p

f
p
pp

Sonata No. 2

(Theme)

JOSEPH HAYDN

Brightly (𝅗𝅥 = 120)*

*Metronome marks 𝅗𝅥 = two beats to a bar.

Sonata No. 5

(Theme)

JOSEPH HAYDN

Brightly (♩ = 152)

ATF105

p
f
p
f

Sonata No. 7

(Theme)

JOSEPH HAYDN

Fast (𝅗𝅥 = 100)*

* Metronome Marks 𝅗𝅥 = two beats to a bar.

Fine
D. C. al Fine

Sonata in A Major

(Theme)

WOLFGANG AMADEUS MOZART

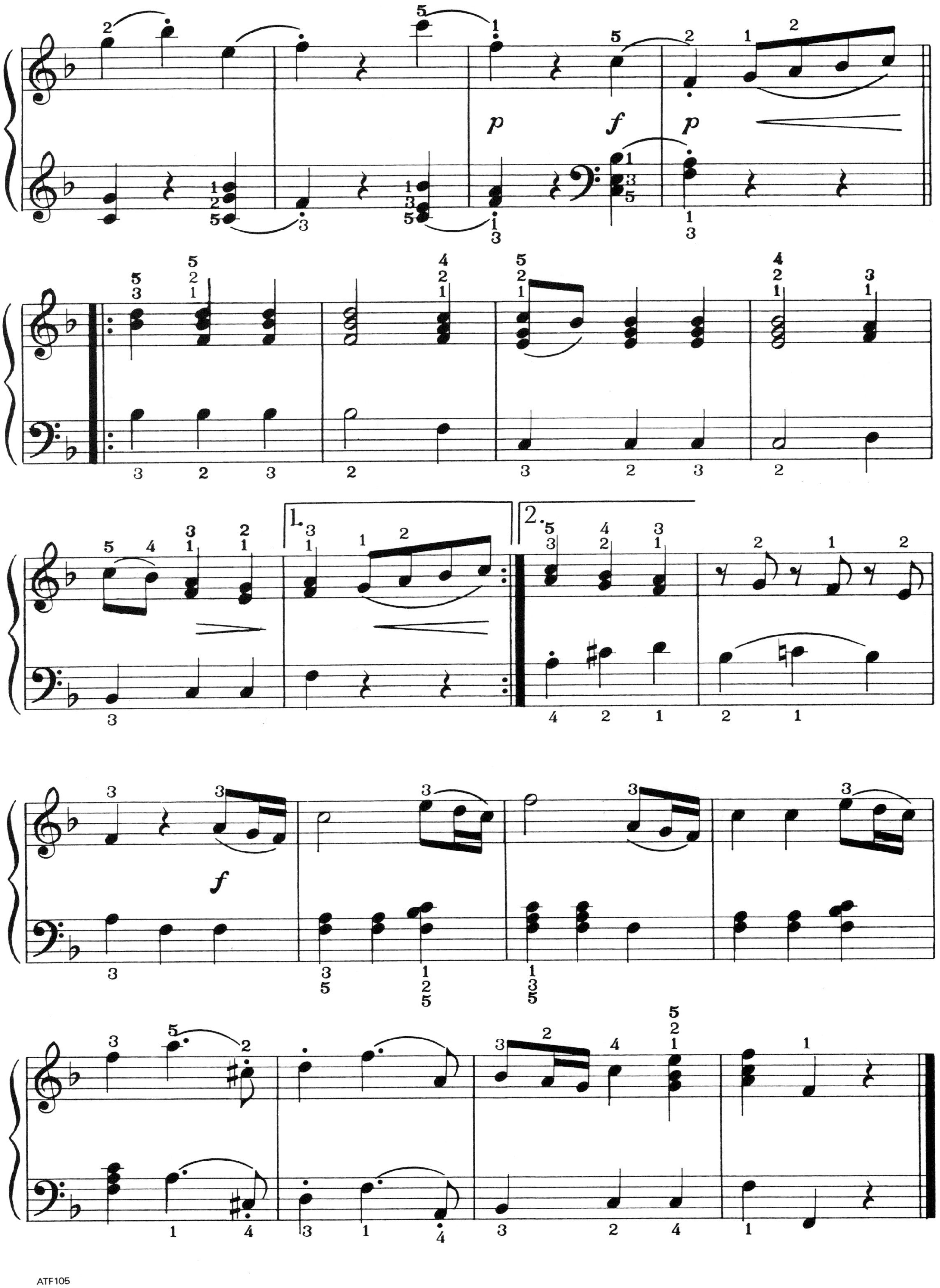

"Jupiter" Symphony

(Theme)

WOLFGANG AMADEUS MOZART, K.551

Quick (♩ = 152)

ff
f
ff
ff

Sonata in C Major

(Theme)

WOLFGANG AMADEUS MOZART, K.545

Brightly (𝅗𝅥 = 132)*

* Metronome Marks 𝅗𝅥 = two beats to a bar.

p
mf

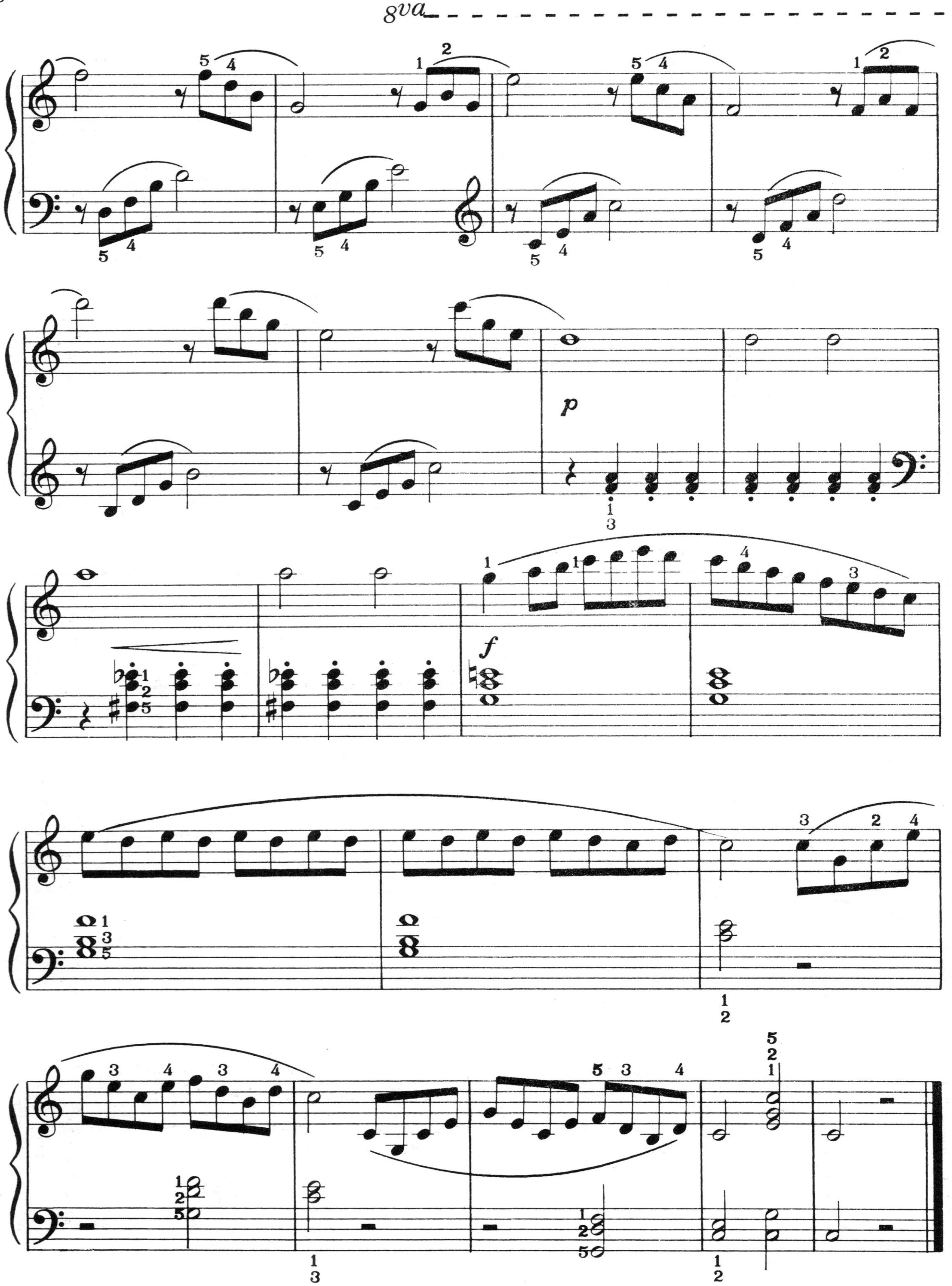
8va
p
f

"Moonlight" Sonata

(Theme)

Slowly (♩ = 56)

LUDWIG van BEETHOVEN

pp

pp

Sonata in G Major

(Theme)

LUDWIG van BEETHOVEN

*Metronome Marks 𝅗𝅥 = two beats to a bar.

Sonatina in G Major

LUDWIG van BEETHOVEN

Moderately fast (♩ = 132)

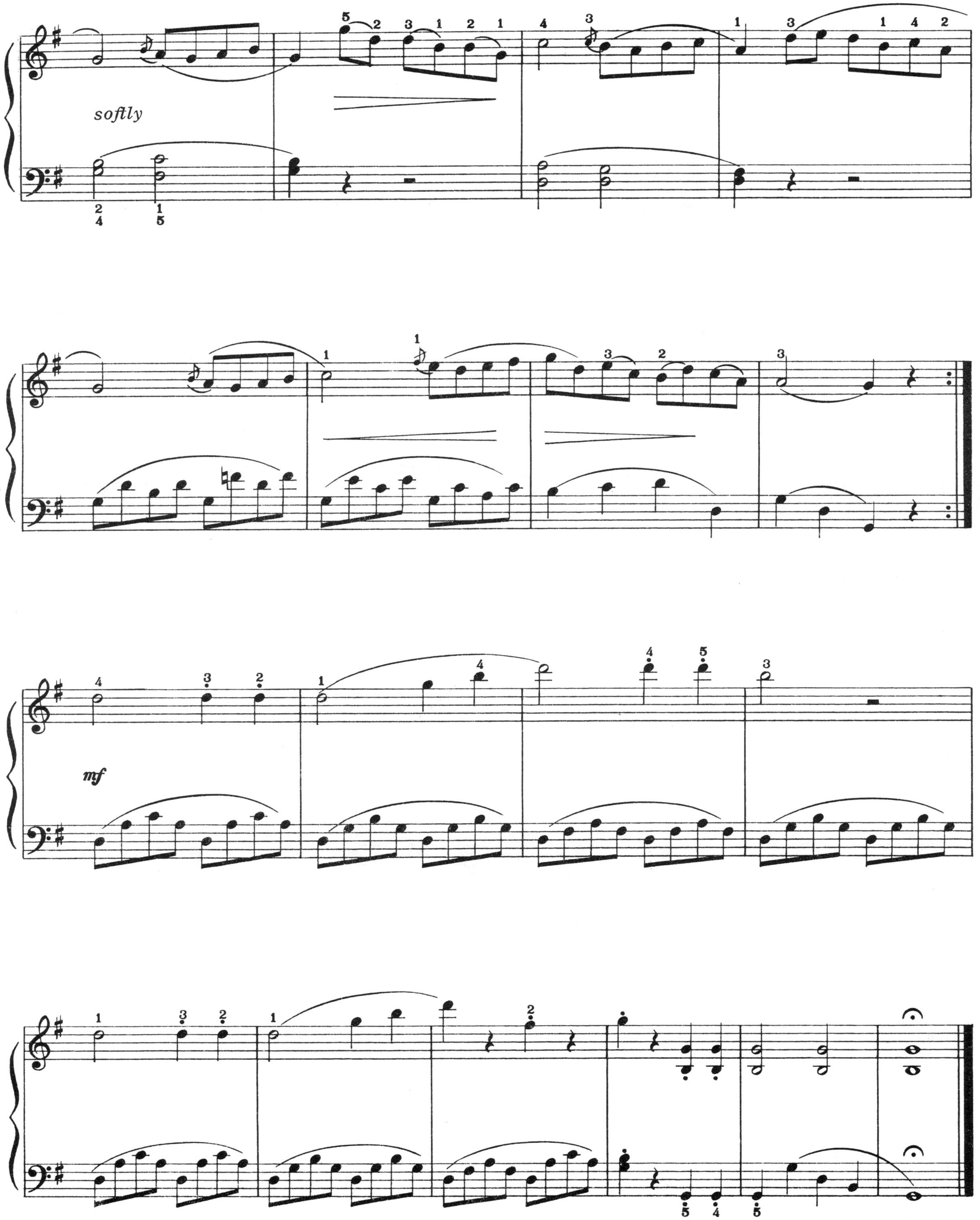
softly
mf

"Emperor" Concerto

(Theme)

LUDWIG van BEETHOVEN

Moderately fast (♩ = 132)

ATF105

A little slower
p
f

Original time
In tempo
f

Symphony No. 5
(Theme)

LUDWIG van BEETHOVEN

Brightly (♩ = 176)

increase in power
ff
ff
ff

ff

Piano Concerto No. 1

(Theme)

FRÉDÉRICK CHOPIN

p
rit.
p
in time

p
f

Symphony in D Minor

(Themes)

CÉSAR FRANCK

* Metronome Marks 𝅗𝅥 = two beats to a bar.

mf
f
f
1.
2.
ff

8va
sfz

Albumleaf

EDVARD GRIEG

Moderately (♩ = 88)

ritard.
p
in tempo

Ase's Death

from *Peer Gynt* Suite No. 1

EDVARD GRIEG

Slowly (♩ = 54)

f
ff
p
p
p

Morning Mood

from *Peer Gynt* Suite No. 1

EDVARD GRIEG

Moderately (♩ = 72)

mf
p
pp

Solvejg's Song

from *Peer Gynt* Suite No. 2

EDVARD GRIEG

Moderately (♩ = 86)

Fine
p
D.C. al Fine

Piano Concerto in A Minor

(Theme)

Brightly (𝅗𝅥 = 96)*

EDVARD GRIEG

* Metronome marks 𝅗𝅥 = two beats to a bar.

ATF105

rit.
in time
More animated
mp lightly
ff

mp
8va
8va
ff

p
somewhat slower
mp in time
mf
f
8va
8va
slightly rit.
p
rit.
Slower
p

pp
pp
sustained
mf
in time
pp
sustained
mp
more animated
f
gradually faster

ff
sf
fz
rit.
mp
In a singing style

rit.
in time
fz
8va
ff
fz
fz
sf

Les Préludes

(Themes)

FRANZ LISZT

f
mf
mf
f

ff
ff
ffz

"New World" Symphony

(Theme)

ANTON DVOŘÁK

Very slow (♩ = 69)

pp
f
pp

p
pp
p
p
pp

Piano Concerto No. 4

(Theme)

ANTON RUBINSTEIN

Moderately (♩ = 104)

A little faster
p with expression

rit.
Original time
f
ff

Ave Maria

FRANZ SCHUBERT

Slowly (♩ = 60)

March Militaire

FRANZ SCHUBERT

March time (in 2 , 𝅗𝅥 = 112)

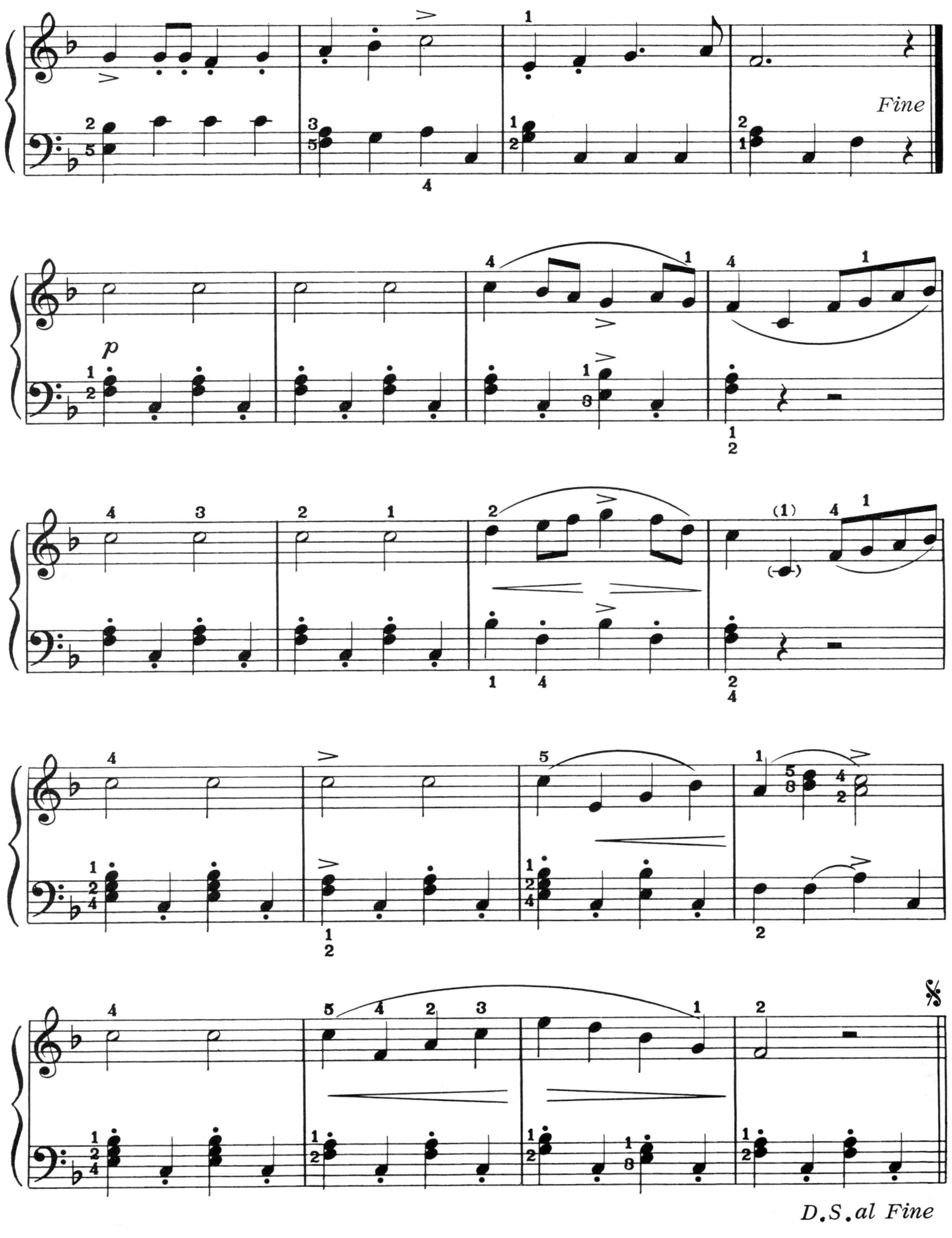
Fine
D.S. al Fine

Ballet Music

from *Rosamunde*

Marchlike (in 2 , 𝅗𝅥 = 92)

FRANZ SCHUBERT

D.C. al Fine

"Unfinished" Symphony

(Theme)

FRANZ SCHUBERT

Moderately fast (♩ = 96)

Serenade

FRANZ SCHUBERT

Moderately (♩ = 69)

Cradle Song

FRANZ SCHUBERT

Slowly with feeling (♩ = 96)

Why?

ROBERT SCHUMANN

Slow and tender (♩ = 60)

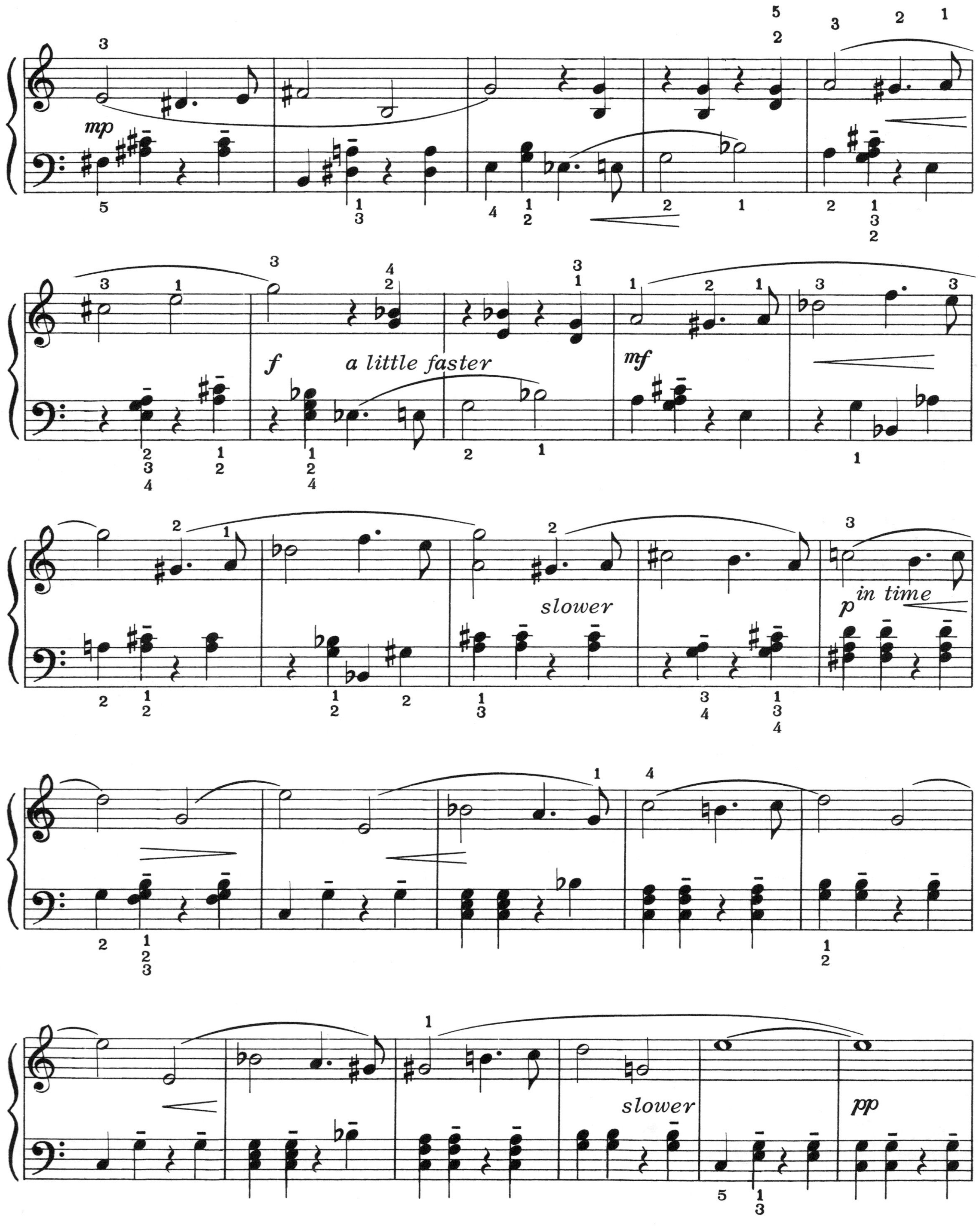
mp
f
a little faster
mf
slower
p
in time
slower
pp

mp in time
mf
f
f
slower
p in time
slower
pp

Cradle Song

Moderately (♩ = 104) **ROBERT SCHUMANN**

mf
Slower
Original tempo
p
pp
pp

Knight Rupert

ROBERT SCHUMANN

f
p

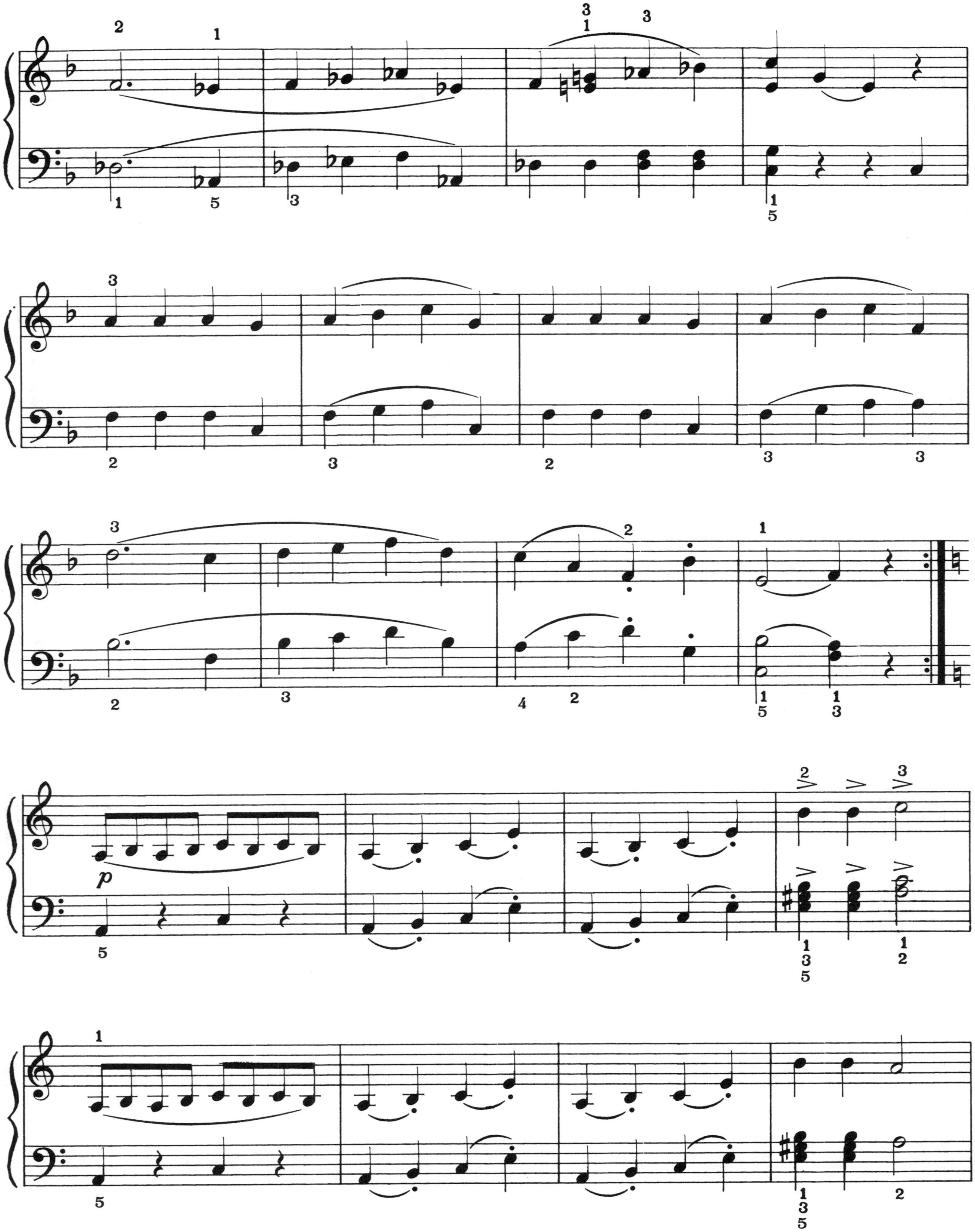
p

The Merry Farmer

In a happy mood (♩ = 120)

ROBERT SCHUMANN

Träumerei

ROBERT SCHUMANN

Romance

ROBERT SCHUMANN

Moderately (♩ = 100)
p
slower
in time mf
slower
in time
slower
p

Capriccio Italian

(Theme)

PETER ILYITCH TCHAIKOVSKY

Easy waltz time

mf
f

Piano Concerto No. 1

(Theme)

Majestic (♩ = 84)

PETER ILYITCH TCHAIKOVSKY

8va
8va
8va
8va
p
pp

Dance of the Swans

from *The Swan Lake* Ballet

PETER ILYITCH TCHAIKOVSKY

p
f

Marche Slav

PETER ILYITCH TCHAIKOVSKY

Moderately-march time

mf
p
pp very softly

Symphony No. 5
(Theme)

PETER ILYITCH TCHAIKOVSKY

Slowly
First time
rit.

Waltz

from *Serenade for Strings*

PETER ILYITCH TCHAIKOVSKY

Pavane
(Theme)

MAURICE RAVEL

Slowly, with expression (♩ = 54)

ATF105

f
p
Very slow
mf
f

Original time
p
rit.
mf
ff

Arabesque No. 1

(Theme)

Moderately (♩ = 100)

CLAUDE DEBUSSY

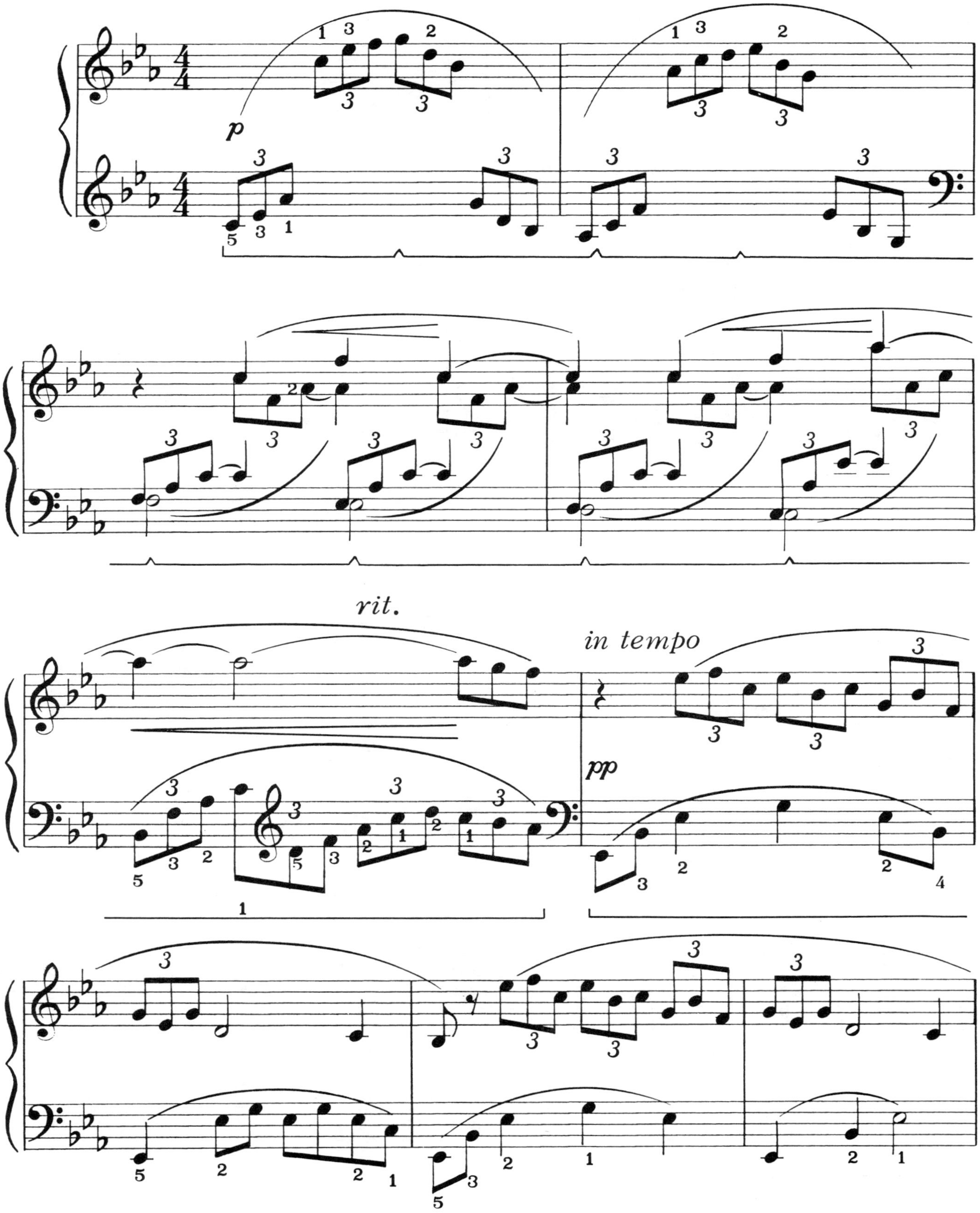

Faster
mf
f
rit.
Slower
p
sf

Original time
rit.
p
p
p
pp
8va
pp

Comedians Gallop

(Theme)

DMITRI KABALEVSKY

Fast (♩ = 200)

Fine
D. C. al fine

Sabre Dance

(Theme)

Fast (♩ = 152)

DMITRI KABALEVSKY

ff
f
ff
Same time
mf
with expression

f

Bear Dance

BÉLA BARTÓK

cresc.
f strongly
Well marked
mf
sf
sf
f

sf
sf
mf
similarly
sf
sf
p

mf
sf
sf
f
sf
mf
gradually increasing in power
f strongly
sf

mf
sf
sf
sf
sf
p
p
gradually
decreasing
sf
p
pp

Ballad

BÉLA BARTÓK

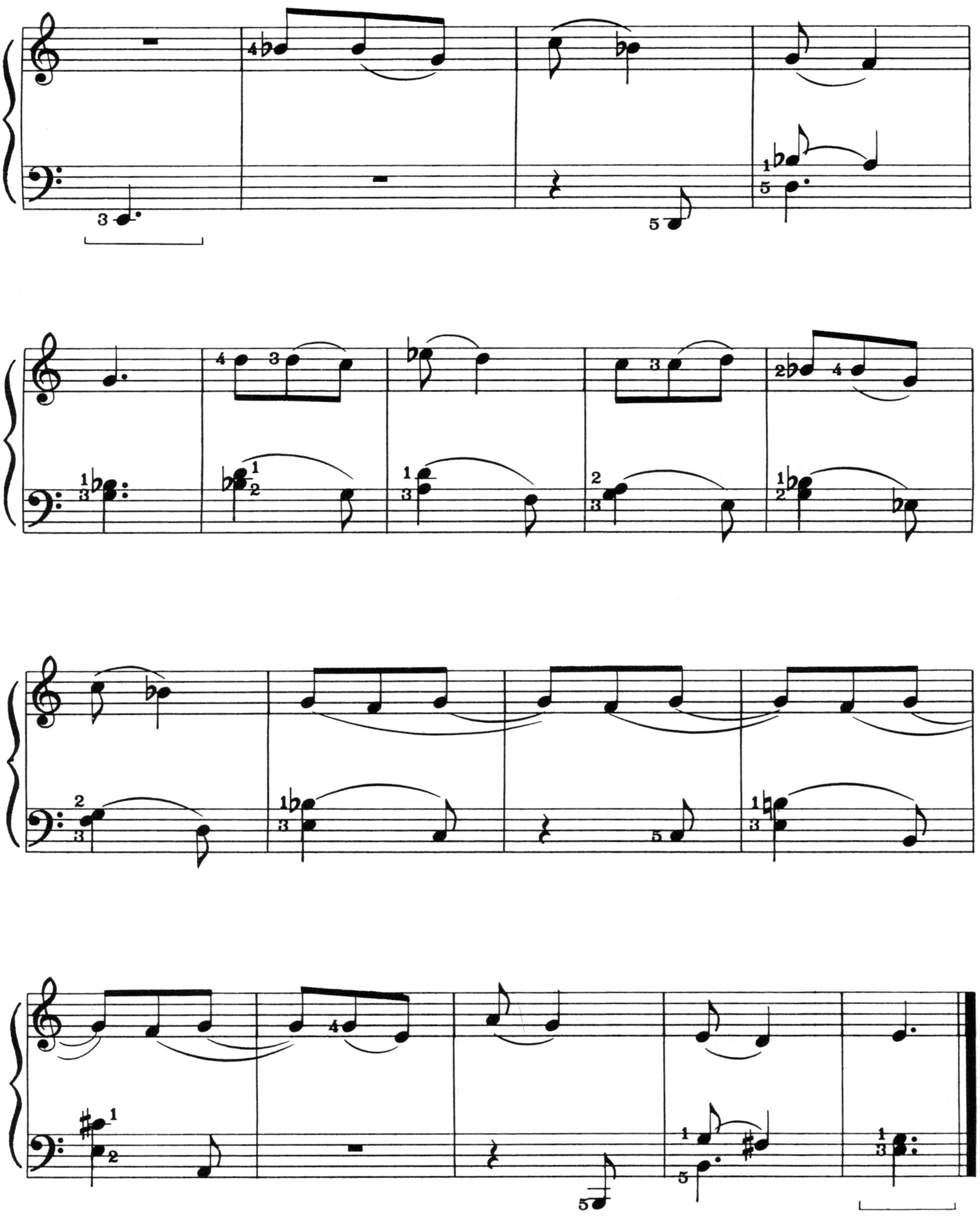

Playing Games

BÉLA BARTÓK

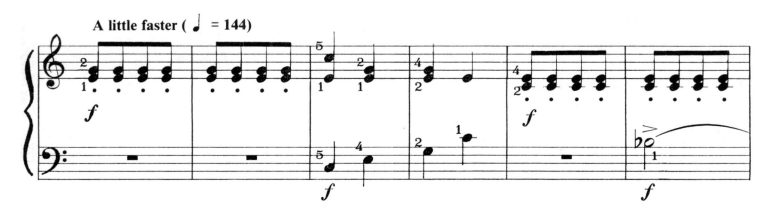

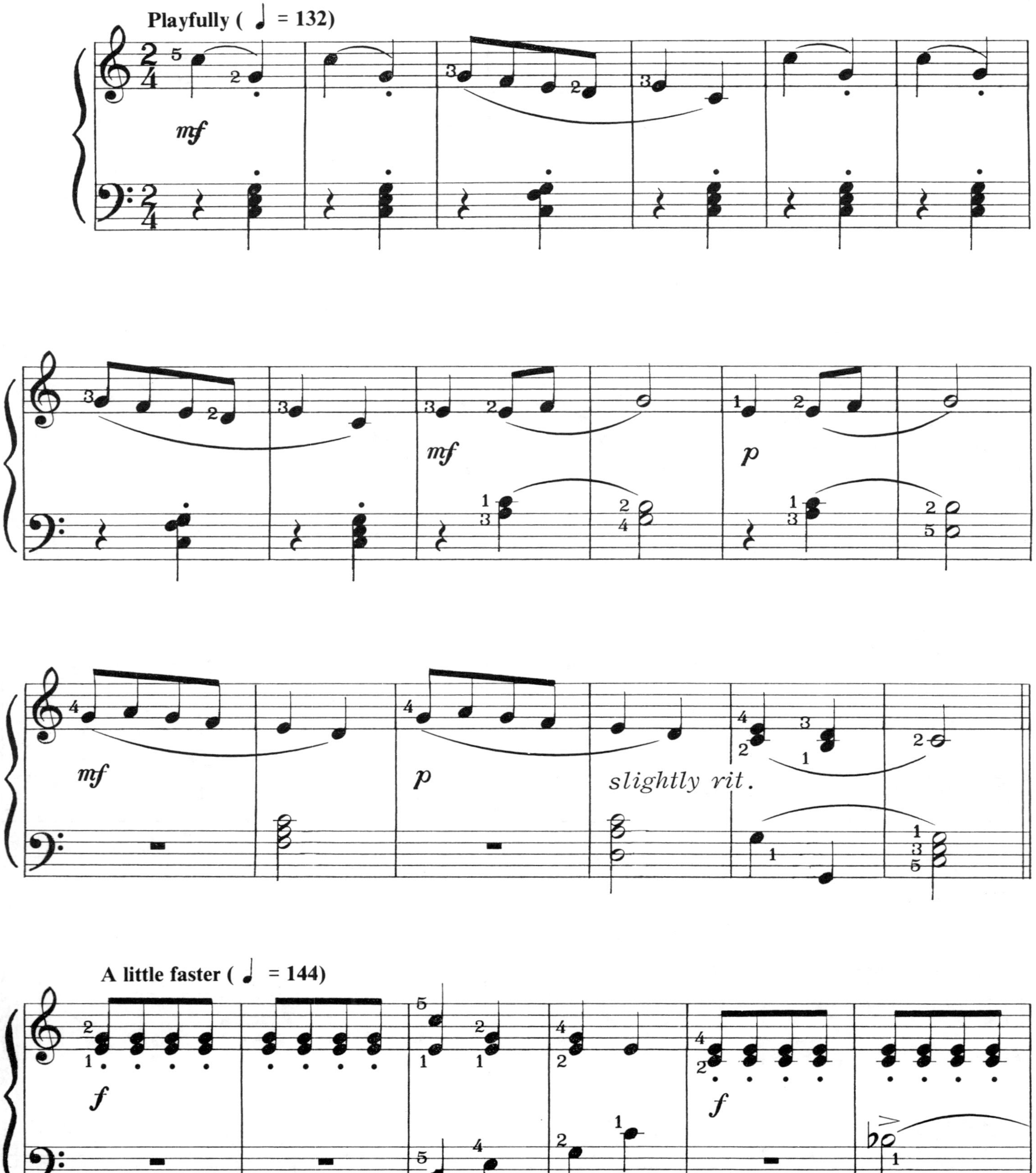

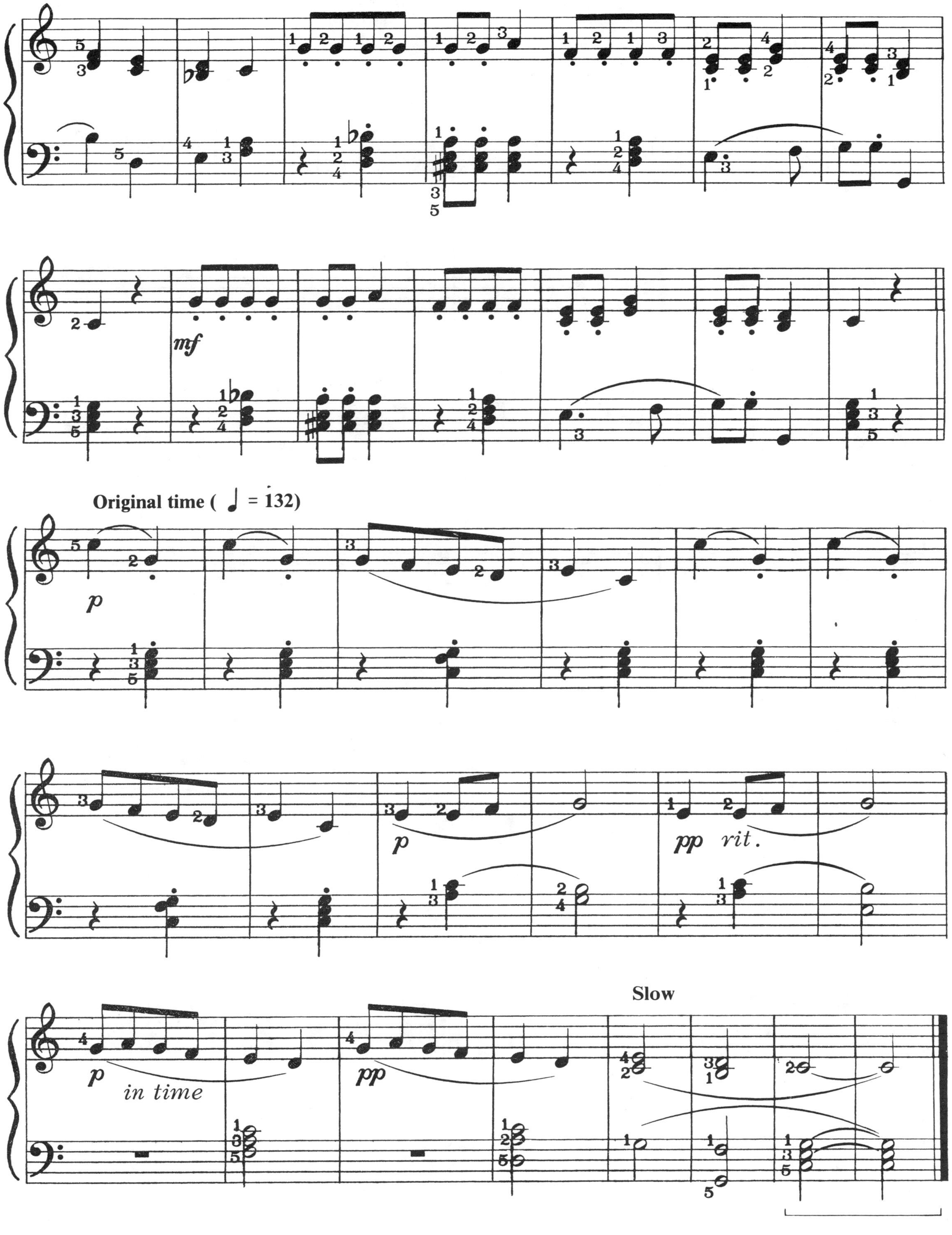
mf
Original time (♩ = 132)
p
p
pp rit.
p
in time
pp
Slow

Gavotte

from *Classical Symphony*

Moderately fast (♩ = 120)

SERGE PROKOFIEFF

1.
2.
mf
f
p
mf
f

March

from the opera *The Love of Three Oranges*

SERGE PROKOFIEFF

ATF105

mf
ff
1.
2.

Once upon a Time

SERGE PROKOFIEFF

Playing Tag

SERGE PROKOFIEFF

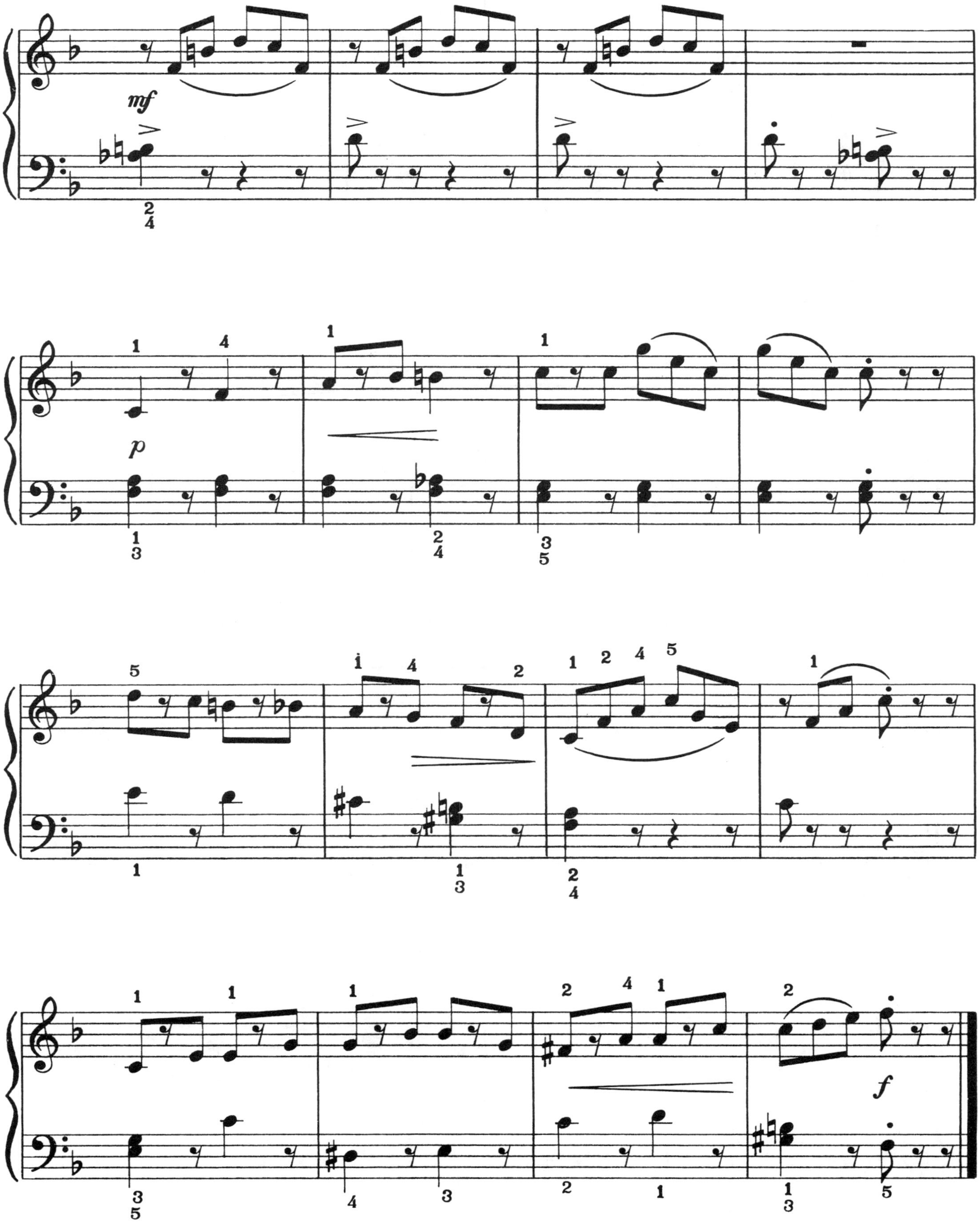
mf
p
f

Gympodie No. 1

(Theme)

ERIC SATIE

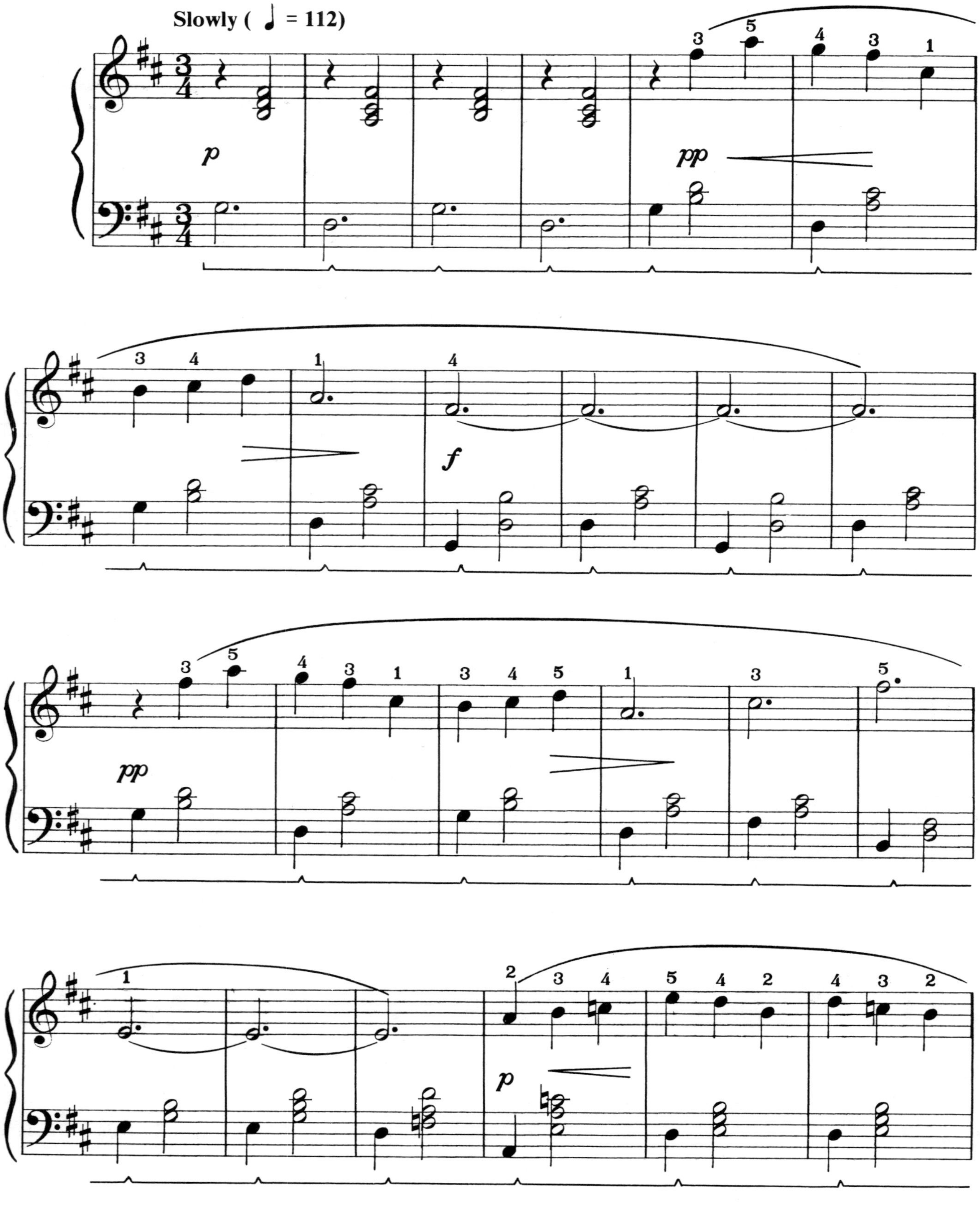

pp
p

Lotus Land

CYRIL SCOTT

Little faster
f
rit.
p *in time*
increasing in time
f

f
p
rit.
in time

mf
p
mf
p
p
pp
p
mf
f
p

Adagio

DMITRI SHOSTAKOVITCH

pp

Festive Waltz

DMITRI SHOSTAKOVITCH

f

Polka

DMITRI SHOSTAKOVITCH

sf
f
p
f

Sad Little Song

DMITRI SHOSTAKOVITCH

Moderately slow

p
pp

Punchinello
(Theme)

HEITOR VILLA-LOBOS

Fast (𝅗𝅥 = 100)

p
ff
ff